PHIL LABOON

AUTOMATE YOUR INCOME

BY

PHIL LABOON

AUTOMATE YOUR INCOME

Copyright © 2020 by Phil Laboon.

All rights reserved. No part of this publication may be reproduced, distributed, or transmitted in any form or by any means, including photocopying, recording, or other electronic or mechanical methods, without the prior written permission of the author, except in the case of brief quotations embodied in critical reviews and certain other noncommercial uses permitted by copyright law.

Ordering Information:

Quantity sales. Special discounts are available on quantity purchases by corporations, associations, and others. Orders by U.S. trade bookstores and wholesalers.

www.DreamStartersPublishing.com

Table of Contents

Dedication 4

Introduction 5

Getting Started in Entrepreneurship 7

What is Automatic Income Streaming? 36

Developing Your Stream 57

Starting Your Journey 75

Building Authority in a Niche 88

Leveraging Your Followers 97

Increasing Life-Time Value (LTV) 112

Miscellaneous Thoughts on Digital Platforms 118

Final Thoughts 122

What Do I Do Now? 124

Testimonials 133

Dedication

No one ever does "everything" alone. Mom and Dad have supported me through every up and down of my entrepreneurial journey. It might have been easier on them if I'd been a doctor or something, but they have never wavered in their belief in me.

I am deeply grateful for a love I can never repay.

Introduction

As entrepreneurs, I think most of us have been misled. We've been told that to be financially successful, we need to take out high-interest loans, hire dozens of employees, and expose ourselves to massive risks – and all for limited rewards. The truth is, in this day and age, anyone with even a minor understanding of technology can surpass what they would make in a nine-to-five job with nothing but a computer and an internet connection. Best of all, they can do it by "barely working." With automated streams of income, the 40, 50 or 60-hour work week is over and done with.

In this book, I'm going to show you, step by step, several unconventional ways to earn long-term, passive monthly income, with little to no out-of-pocket expenses. You don't have to go broke to make money. You don't need to put yourself in debt to start a business. With the ideas contained here, you'll be able to earn six-figures, from home.

If you're an entrepreneur looking for extra income, I've written this book for you. If you're a CEO or upper-management professional who feels overworked and underpaid, this book is for you, too. If you've tried to make money selling MLM products, you've probably noticed there aren't enough people who want your product. Instead you have to recruit, recruit, recruit, and usually buy your own inventory to see any profit.

If you're just starting, you can learn from my mistakes (which I'll outline in detail) and make money passively. You can jump off the negative, draining cycles involved in most start-ups and in building new income streams by using the tips and techniques in this book. You can start with no money down, no employees, and no investment other than your time. You can grow a business that will help you make over six figures each year.

Come on - fire your boss and start building your own passive income – today!

Chapter 1

Getting Started in Entrepreneurship

Every school has "a hustler" – the kid who always has something going on the side. Maybe he sells gum or candy on the playground – maybe she negotiates the best trades in the lunchroom. But, every school has one.

In my school, that kid was me. For as long as I can remember, entrepreneurism has pumped through my veins and been my true north. Ever since I was old enough to carry a shovel, I spent snow days clearing walkways and driveways. When the weather was clear, I knocked on doors selling wrapping paper to win school fundraisers. While others in my grade were obsessing over Ninja Turtles and the WWF (World Wrestling Federation), I was trying to create businesses –

even though I did not know it. My mindset has sent me down the unique path I continue to travel today.

While I'm pretty sure you didn't buy this book to read about how I sold thousands of Hostess pies in the hallways of my high school, I think it's important for me to share a little history so you can see how my brain is wired. You can get an idea of the mental approach needed to recognize automated income opportunities. These chances present themselves to you all the time. But, unless you can identify them and recognize them for what they are, they will zoom past you like trucks on the Interstate.

Luck does not exist – scientifically proven. Good things and bad things happen to all of us. When good things happen, it's not simply good fortune. Instead, what other people call "luck" happens when "opportunity" runs head-first into "preparation." Luck involves your mindset – being motivated toward a specific vision or goal, and making decisions, big and small, that will help you reach it. In this book, we'll talk about how to harness luck in a way that generates true financial independence.

The first real business I started was during my opening week in high school. I noticed some kids selling ridiculously overpriced lollipops. While you were not allowed to eat candy during class, kids were shelling out $1 for something you could buy at the store for 25 cents. *I gotta get in on this.*

I appropriated my dad's oversized cooler lunch box and filled it with various things I thought my classmates would want. I remember cramming in cans of soda, candy bars, gum, and Hostess snack cakes. On the bus, I kept fretting about my stuff being confiscated.

Before the beginning of class, I'd crack open a can of Coke with as much flourish as possible. The *pfffffft* of the soda announced: "I am open for business." It didn't take long for word to get out that "the Phil kid" had a ready supply of "eats" on hand. Before I knew it, I was selling $20-30 a day at a decent mark-up. Since my prior jobs involved – you know – work (shoveling driveways in winter, raking leaves in fall, or helping my dad as a laborer on construction jobs in the summer), handing over treats while classmates shoved dollar bills in my face was much more enjoyable.

All good things end. After a few weeks, I was called to the Principal's office. While I could tell he respected the hustle, I was informed I could no longer sell snacks during school hours. Most 14-year-old kids probably would have sucked up their losses and let it go, but I was a problem solver. I was not going down without a fight.

"What about the other kids selling candy?"

"They are raising money for a school-sponsored sport," he said.

Light bulb! I knew what I had to do. Before I left school that day, I went to the office to find out how to start a school-sponsored sport. Over the next few weeks, I followed all the steps and created the first ever "Ultimate Frisbee Team" at my school. Once we were recognized by the Administration, I was back in business. I upgraded the operation – brought multiple coolers and had other kids selling for me for a percentage of profits. At my peak, I was buying half pallet loads of "almost expired" Hostess snack cakes that I stored in my parents' garage.

Of course, I got called to the Principal's office again, but when I explained we were fundraising for new uniforms – checkmate! I had him and he knew it. I ran my business during all four years of high school. After I graduated, a younger student took it over and used the same model.

As I got older I recognized my unique worldview. I always look at the bigger picture. While most of my classmates were driven to get good grades so they could go to a better college and make money, I was looking for how to eliminate the middleman (i.e. four or nine years of college). I wanted to make money – right then! My focus on schooling all but died. All I thought about was business.

While I worked after school at Long John Silvers, Brueggers Bagels, and a sign company, I was always thinking: *Why am I working to make someone else money?* or *Why should this company benefit more from my hard work than I do?*

My First Side Hustles

While I had a lot of jobs, the first side hustle I ever created was at 16 when I landed a position making vinyl signs and decals. Basically, I pulled vinyl letters off large rolls and put them on different signage materials. It was a very small business – just the manager and me. He was a younger guy who played in a punk rock band, so I didn't endure much day-to-day oversight.

After a while, I realized the expensive part of the signs was not the vinyl; it was the software, the cutter, and the experience that allowed us to charge the prices we did. Once I had a solid understanding of the entire process, I started ordering my own vinyl rolls and soliciting side business with local companies. I made banners for DJs, magnet signs for work trucks, and yard signs for contractors. I can still remember how intimidating it was to walk into a business filled with older construction guys and try to sell them on why they needed new vinyl signs for their trucks.

What stands out most to me about the experience is that it felt real. I was still a kid, but I was making money like an adult. Grownups weren't selling candy or shoveling driveways, but they did sell signs. I felt like I was entering an actual career, and it ultimately led me to pursue training in Multimedia Design.

The reason I am starting with these examples is to give you a glimpse into my mindset and what it takes to be successful in this world. You need to accept risk, overcome obstacles, and think outside of the box if you want to make your own path as an entrepreneur. Good grades are nice, but they do not ultimately matter. (Remember, I was not trying to get into Harvard Law.) I was a terrible student, and didn't grow up with any privilege. I made my own success without relying on anyone else. At the same time, I'm a bit of a maverick who doesn't take "no" for an answer. Sometimes I found success; sometimes I fell on my face. But, hitting an obstacle simply made me look for a way to overcome it.

Recreational Equipment

When I finished school, I took an entry-level position as an assistant to the CEO of a 40+ year old recreational equipment company. Realizing that if I ever wanted to leave my parents' basement I would need to make more than minimum wage; I convinced the owner to let me build a website in my spare time and get paid a percentage of each sale I generated.

Once he agreed, I was hooked. Back in 2002, the possibilities were endless and the internet was an affiliate marketer's paradise. Using tactics that would make contemporary digital marketers cringe, I generated massive amounts of free, organic traffic in weeks. After getting the site to rank for hundreds of competitive phrases like "Football Equipment" and "Discount Sporting Goods," I shot into the lead as the top salesperson in the company.

What was crazy is that once I got the rankings, it didn't take much time out to keep them. Even if I did nothing, I generated a fair amount of sales. I leveraged my new-found value to the company into an increased base salary and an agreement to allow me to work from home three days a week. In a matter of months, I went from making less than a McDonald's manager to bringing in almost $50,000 – part-time.

My friends and family members were amazed to discover I was not as dumb as I looked. I held the job for a year and a half. Then the owner realized he could fire me and keep *all* the profits. Honestly, though, I didn't even care; I had aspirations of being the next Bill Gates.

Breathalyzer Keychains

With a year-and-a-half of eCom marketing under my belt, I thought I was ready to start my own company, one that would change the world. I had lost three friends to drinking and driving within two years, so I thought I had the perfect idea: a keychain breathalyzer you could use to stop a friend from driving drunk.

I initiated my LLC and started contacting Chinese suppliers to get my revolutionary product off the ground only to find out there was already an established competitor several steps ahead of me. Good news – it didn't have any marketing abilities, so I couldn't find anything about them online. I contacted the owner after a manufacturer gave me his info and we hit it off. He was twice my age and had decades of experience. We agreed to team up and dominate the market.

My job was creating all the online marketing materials and sales; he handled logistics. I went to work optimizing the website and leveraging my edge to get a massive amount of local and national press. We grew quickly, but insurmountable manufacturing issues eventually drove us to close our doors.

I'm not going to lie – I felt like I'd been punched in the stomach. I had invested a huge amount of time and money in the business, and as soon as we hit our stride, we boarded up the windows. I needed another reliable revenue stream and I needed it fast.

Organic SEO / Link Building

At this point, I had made hundreds of thousands of dollars in eCom sales and understood the SEO industry better than anyone else around. I decided to start a small digital marketing consultancy and get paid for my hard-earned knowledge.

Like most businesses, things started off slowly. I ranked #1 for all the keywords related to Pittsburgh Digital Marketing, but no one was searching for them. Back then, people thought the only way to get more online business was to build a cooler animated flash page. I tried selling websites for reasonable prices, but no businesses built their companies via the web back then, so a 22-year-old kid asking for $5,000 to build a website went nowhere.

Running out of money, I put on the business suit my parents bought for my senior high school pictures and started knocking on doors. I sold full websites for $199. (Yep, $199!) I figured if I could get folks to sign up for a low fee, I could upsell them other services like hosting, marketing, business cards, etc. To my surprise, it worked and I had a business model that didn't rely on anyone else. I was the sole owner.

Like the USPS, neither snow nor rain nor heat nor gloom of night stopped me from knocking on doors with promises of internet fame and fortune. Sales rolled in fast and I started recruiting more commission-based salespeople to make the visits and sell, sell, sell. Everything was perfect except for one thing: I only knew how to make basic websites, and they were not very good. I was a marketing guy not a developer, so I needed a way to get all the sites built – on the cheap.

I made a deal with a guy in India. (We met in one of my marketing forums.) We used cheap templates (thanks, Template Monster) and streamlined a process to churn out a website in hours. Over the next year, because of my rankings, our phones rang off the hook. It was time to take the business to the next level.

I worked night and day on SEO processes and my new partner hired implementation people in his country at a fraction of the U.S. cost. Don't get me wrong – the work was high quality. They followed the instructions to a "T" and since we paid on "jobs completed" (instead of by the hour), workers had incentive to get the work done – fast!

This was my first real profitable AIS (Automated Income Stream). I just had to answer the phone, make the sale, and send the information to my team. My associates handled 100% of the work. At twenty-three, I was making six-figures of passive income and ready for my next AIS.

Pre-construction Real Estate Boom

I thought I was invincible. I was a kid who barely graduated high school, got kicked out of his first college after two weeks, and had several run-ins with police. (You don't need all the gory details - I didn't do anything *really* bad.)

I was now making more money than most of my friends' parents and a hell of a lot more than any of my buddies. I'm surprised I could fit my enlarged head into my used Nissan 350-Z I bought on Craigslist.

While my parents were on vacation, they met a real estate guy who told them what was happening in the market. He said people were buying homes that weren't even built yet. The brokers were selling out whole developments in hours. My parents told him about my company and we connected. It was a match made in heaven. The broker needed leads and I needed a new automated income, so we created a 50/50 partnership.

Using a few techniques that could be called "Growth Hacks," we made massive waves overnight. The first technique was using a piece of software I built with a friend that allowed us to post in the real estate sections of classified sites where we prospected for investors. I was proud of myself because no one had figured out how to post. My approach was not sophisticated – I "duct-taped" together a technique using dozens of used computers from Goodwill and utilizing old school dial-up modems to get around IP addresses.

Because the housing developments weren't built yet, we could rank for their names and locations in a matter of days. The developers had spent millions on traditional marketing but had *no websites* for traffic. We zoomed to the top in ranking.

We also built an educational hub for real estate investors looking for more information. We got all the scoop on the developments and gave our thoughts on the best ones. We also highlighted on up-and-coming areas and outlined the tax incentives were in the pipeline. By providing a high level of value, we ranked #1 for hundreds of the most competitive keywords. Within 30 days, we had 20+ full-time agents. We were generating hundreds of real estate leads a day from our rankings and the money (at least on paper) was beyond amazing. There were days that we were making more than I made the entire previous year. It almost seemed too good to be true.

Guess what? It was!

You see, we did not get paid until the development was built and 90% of the developments were never completed. I was left holding the bag for a massive amount of advertising fees and employees. Throw in the fact that my "partner" took everything from our bank account and you can see, I was in a world of hurt. It took ten years of court battles to get even a portion of my money back.

A major crash and burn.

Short-Term Vacation Rentals

After the 2008 recession hit and I lost hundreds of thousands of dollars in my real estate brokerage, I decided to use my new knowledge (and the last of my credit) to buy some rental houses. At the time there weren't many short-term vacation rental websites, so I built my own sites and marketed on my own through free classified sites. It was a lot of work but the ROI was really strong, especially considering I was picking up homes for a fraction of what they were worth.

Wooden eCom Products

While the breathalyzer keychain business was my first true eCom company, WUDN was by far my most successful.

I did marketing for dozens of eCom companies and I thought it was time to take a stab at building my own brand. I met a young ambitious guy who had a great idea: buy pre-existing, cheap products and slap a wood veneer on them. It was genius! I invested $20,000 to buy materials and a laser cutter and we were quickly up and running.

At first we thought we would be more of a promotional products company, but we quickly discovered a massive potential in the market: cell phone battery cases. There were hundreds of battery cases on the market, but they were all cheap, ugly plastic. We researched, found the best model, slapped some wood on it, and our life changed. We couldn't manufacture and ship fast enough.

An ad I shot in my backyard went viral and generated tens of thousands of views a day. We had a back order of thousands of phones within weeks. The first year out of the gate we had several hundred thousand in sales with a 90%+

profit margin. Unfortunately, I had no clue how deadly the logistics would be. If I wanted to take this business to the next level, I needed to make a significant investment in a larger facility, more employees, a larger stock of inventory, etc., which just wasn't for me.

I sold the company to a telecom executive.

The Entrepreneur's Mindset: Overcoming Fear

Everyone with a new business venture gets a little scared – and they should be. In fact, if you aren't a little nervous or scared, you should stop whatever it is you're doing because you aren't going in with your eyes and brain open to what might happen, good or bad. Take a step back, and examine the situation. Recalculate to ensure you're factoring everything in before you get started.

It's natural to be frightened – you're most likely doing something you've never done before. I was lucky. Since I'd been making money since high school, I knew I could do it. Side hustles were as much a part of me as breathing.

But, I made the mistake that a lot of entrepreneurs make. When I began to doubt my instincts, I pulled in a partner who "knew what he was doing." It burned me almost every time.

Turns out, I was afraid to do something on my own. A lot of young entrepreneurs make the same mistake – they scramble for a partner because they think they need somebody else to find success. And, like me, more often than not, it falls apart – either because the partner really doesn't help out, the partner hurts the business, or the partner steals ideas or money, either directly or indirectly.

My partner in my breathalyzer keychain business was much older – more established in the business world. In my inexperience, I assumed he would be an asset. And, in some ways, he was. You can learn from almost anyone. He had already done some of the footwork when it came to manufacturing, and he possessed valuable business experience.

But, the venture ultimately failed on his side. I was leading marketing and sales; he handled manufacturing. And his area bombed. We fell apart in the very areas where I thought he would cover us. It was a valuable lesson.

I learned not to be afraid of going it alone. I also lost my fear of failure. We learn when things go sideways. If we pay attention to the reasons for failure, we get better.

I learned that failure isn't the end. It's just part of the process toward success. Instead of getting hung up on avoiding failure, I instead say to myself, "Okay, I failed/screwed up. What did I learn? Let's move on!"

Some people say, "Well, if it doesn't work out, it's not meant to be." They give up too quickly – I think out of fear. Sometimes, they are too scared to start.

I'm an entrepreneur through and through. I keep pushing. Even if you have a great company and you are making six-figures in a secure job, you can (and should) still pursue automated income streams like an e-course, or eCom services.

A friend of mine worked hard at becoming a well-respected Instagram influencer. She was making decent money and lived in a low-cost area. Working part-time as an influencer brought in between $70,000 and $80,000 a year.

She wanted to up her game, so she took three months to develop a nice e-course that included a step-by-step guide. She marketed with a free webinar where she explained what she was going to teach: how to become an Instagram influencer. In the first month of offering the e-course, she made more money than she had the entire previous year. She now has follow-up courses on how to become a speaker, appear on local news programs as an "expert," and more. She's making seven-figures, selling her e-courses, and consulting. If she had remained content – never would have happened.

Even after I analyze skills and personality set, 90% of folks will not make an initial move. They have found a comfort zone. They're accustomed to a certain – they don't want to take a risk. Think about it. If you are making $100,000 a year and spending $95 grand, are you secure? Shouldn't you consider "stretching" a little to increase your net (aka "real") income?

Impatience gets another eight percent. They take the first step. But, when they don't see a lot of money in the first few months, they will declare "failure" and quit. They think, "Well, I tried that – it didn't work." They assume the situation isn't for them and will walk away from an amazing opportunity.

The final two percent latch on and make it work. They keep hustling – they do what they need to do, every day, to build things, to grow their brand, to market their product or service, and to expand their business. They do this, I think, because they're brave. They will not let fear stand in their way. When the results "aren't there" in the first few months, they keep moving and moving – they keep learning. They figure out how to avoid mistakes and how to maximize opportunities.

And they make it work!

The mindset of failing, failing, failing, learning, failing again, learning more, and continuing to learn through all stages of your business. I see the same pattern among all successful entrepreneurs. I started AIS entrepreneurship out of necessity. I had no start-up capital or credit to launch a traditional business. What I'm teaching you in the book I've done many times. I've made a million mistakes, but I've also learned and grown from those" mistakes" and "failures." How many times have I succeeded?

Not really sure - but it's *at least* one more time than I have failed!

I cannot say it too often: Prepare - Work - Follow through - Persist. The number one reason you won't make one of these systems work for you is that you will talk yourself out of it. So, some of you, the biggest risk you will take is reading this book. I'm not trying some "reverse mind Ninja" thing here – I am talking to you from years of experience.

We live in a world of instant gratification. Geez. Until February 14, 2005, we'd never heard of YouTube. Now, we freak out if the video freezes for five seconds.

The thought of investing time challenges a lot of people. Please understand: the annoying voice in the back of your head – the one saying, "It shouldn't take this long" – will never go away. You must learn to ignore it – to smash it – to bury it.

I am not telling you to ignore your own intelligence or to bypass warning signs. Just remain positive and focused. You *are* on the right path.

One of the smartest things I ever did was invest in the Young Entrepreneur Council, an invitation-only support and resource organization. At first, I was looking for the companionship of talking with other entrepreneurs. My hometown of Pittsburgh suffered from a serious lack of young entrepreneurs. No one was doing anything groundbreaking. There were many "wantrepreneurs" (ambitious dreamers who talked the talk but couldn't walk the walk), but there were very few entrepreneurs whose energy would feed me. Once I joined the YEC, I was hooked, I found myself leaving every event re-energized and with a new passion to create.

Initially, I also joined the YEC for backlinks. Since I was in the internet marketing business, backlinks are very valuable. When you joined, at the time I became a member, you would get links of your business on highly regarded (and high-traffic) websites like *Huffington Post* and *Forbes*. So, at first I thought my membership would be a little side "trick" where I could make money for my clients reselling the backlink service. I wasn't a big believer in groups or meetups, but I soon made some great friends, people with whom I talk daily.

Through other members, I learned the power of networking, sharing ideas and collaboration. It helped me hone my mindset, to prepare for successes and failures, and to anticipate next-steps, including exit strategies. I talk to more of my YEC friends, none of whom live where I live (Pittsburgh), more than to any of my friends locally. We're all in the same mindset; I relate to the questions they have. They understand my struggles, concerns, and dreams.

Surrounding yourself with people of the same mindset of entrepreneurship and life goals will be very beneficial to you as you travel a new path.

AUTOMATE YOUR INCOME

Suppose you have a legal situation or a patent issue. You can throw questions out and get answers based on the collective experience and knowledge of the group. My friends are all smart, and they have all gone through similar experiences, even if they're in a completely different industry from me. They're business owners, entrepreneurs, CEOs who are typically very open with giving advice and counsel. It's a wonderful way to gain support while you navigate every issue you encounter.

As entrepreneurs and business owners, we wear a lot of different hats. Groups like YEC connect you with people who are specialists in different areas. You'll find folks in manufacturing, production, distribution, legal, shipping, and the service industry. If they don't know something, they know someone who has the answer.

You will get great advice and you will build your own virtual team without the chains of having an official "partner." I have a long, long list of colleagues and friends who have become a part of my team. For example, John Hall introduced me to the YEC, and thanks to him I have wonderful advisers. Patrick Barnville and I talk every day; he runs a big eCom company selling lanyards on Amazon. Another colleague, Doran NC, is an amazing developer who builds out websites for me. He does a lot of my programming and technical back-end. Michael Hu owns everything related to accounting – an amazing outsourced CFO. He analyzes my expenses and tells me if I'm in a good financial spot. Ian Blair, another great individual, helps me with app development and mobile presence.

You can find your own people. You can build an amazing team!

Research & Due Diligence

I have seen many people fail by jumping in too quickly without understanding what all was involved. They killed their confidence and their business. When you lead with your heart, it's nearly impossible to forecast timetables or create milestones that are imperative to stay on task and trek forward into the unknown. *Before* you start working on the service you are going to offer, whiteboard everything you need to go live, and how you are going to get it done. Trust me, this will help your brain view this as a real venture. When you reach a milestone, you will feel great.

Here are some of the questions you should be asking yourself:

Am I technology savvy enough to build a quick website in a plug-and-play platform, or am I going to hire it out? Will I use a freelancer or an agency?

Who is going to write the content for the website and emails? Are there similar businesses I can use for inspiration to write for myself?

Do I understand basic accounting or do I need help?

Do I know how to use QuickBooks? Do I know what state and federal taxes I need to pay?

Am I going to start multiple AIS's under one LLC, or will I build a new one for each to decrease liability?

At what point will I need to hire a virtual assistant to help with the workload? When am I going to start interviewing?

Set Goals & Timelines

There is an old saying that pops in my head every time I think of starting a new venture: "Those who fail to plan, plan to fail." Once you finish the due diligence and business model, you must set a realistic timeline. Otherwise you risk falling into "progress limbo."

While everyone's will be different, here are the basic elements you should work into your timeline:

Business Model – A 40,000- foot overview/perspective of your business from start to finish.

Budget Plan – How much money are you willing to invest in this venture?

Mentor Possibility – Do you have anyone that would be willing to mentor you in the industry or business in general?

Competitor Analysis – Complete breakdown of competitors' businesses i.e. pricing, offering, email funnels, add-ons, upsells, etc.

Market Analysis – Do people want your service? Are they willing to pay what you need to charge? How many people are searching online for it?

Elevator Pitch – If you can't quickly explain your model in two sentences, you are going to have a hard time selling it.

Website Content – What is the message you are giving on your website? Are you providing value to the visitor or just providing fluff content?

Email Content – What call to actions are you using in your email sequence? Is your messaging exciting or does it annoy your subscribers?

Bank Account – Do you have a business bank account?

Merchant Account – Can you accept online payments? What processor has the best rates?

QuickBooks Setup – Did you correctly set up QuickBooks for the business? Do you understand the software well enough, come tax time?

Build a Support Network

Unless you are already rubbing shoulders with successful business owners and entrepreneurs, your current group of friends will probably hurt more than help you during inevitable rough patches. Your friends might be incredible human beings, but unless they know, first-hand, the emotional roller coaster that is involved when starting a business from scratch, they won't be able to provide much comfort. There are going to be times when you need someone to give you feedback on something you are too close to evaluate with a clear head. You will need real constructive criticism, not just someone telling you it's going to be okay.

Here are some of the best ways I know how to build a support system:

Join a Business Entrepreneur Group: For many, joining an online entrepreneur group presents one of the easiest ways to meet others in a similar situation. Typically, these groups have forums where you can ask questions without feeling judged, vent about clients, or rant about ridiculous government regulations. A strong bond develops among people facing the same challenges.

Go to Fundraisers: Many successful people want to give back, and most are at least involved with a charity (if not running one themselves). I have met some amazing entrepreneurs and business leaders at fundraising events simply by striking up a conversation in the lobby. The hard part for most people is feeling comfortable and confident enough to talk to a stranger, but if you can gather up the courage (after a drink or two) the pay-off can be huge.

Industry Facebook Groups: Thinking of starting a marketing service? Join the largest marketing Facebook groups you can find. From my experience, the majority of members are business owners and entrepreneurs in the industry. This is a great way to meet others in the industry.

Pretty soon you will have a network of regulars you will chat with daily.

What to Avoid

There are no shortcuts to wealth. Yes, I outline "easy" ways to make passive income via automatic income streams, but that doesn't mean you're going to be able to set up a website, hit a button, lean back in your chair, and watch your bank account grow. Likewise, there are people who make money by working very hard, but I do not recommend their practices: namely, multi-level marketing schemes.

These business structures are predatory, targeting single moms, stay at home parents, families that are struggling, and people who don't have the skills (or don't know how to develop the skills) to start their own businesses. The MLM upline members will tell you it's not a pyramid scheme, or that their organization is "different." The truth is, the vast majority of participants, almost 95% or higher, *lose* money in these schemes. The only people who earn money, a lot of money, are riding on the backs of their downline – that's the real product – not the overpriced leggings, essential oils, or "magic" shakes.

Also, run away from any "investments" that are just schemes in disguise. All of the strategies I discuss in this book are about building your own business, not tying into someone else's "great idea." For every honest idea out there, there are 10,000 scams. Avoid them – you *can* build your own successful AIS business! You will have to work hard, and you (and only you) are responsible for your own success and failure. More than anything else, your work ethic, and what you put into it, will determine how well you do.

Let's take a look now at what exactly I mean by AIS, and how you can start taking some first steps toward creating your own passive (or almost passive) income.

Reflection

What was your first side hustle?

_____

_____

What did you learn from it, and how can you apply those lessons to your current approach?

_____

_____

_____

_____

How has your mindset impacted your success?

_____

_____

_____

_____

"The best marketing strategy ever: Care."

Gary Vaynerchuk

Chapter 2

What is Automatic Income Streaming?

Why don't more people engage in Automatic Income Streaming (AIS)? I think the biggest roadblock is that people think it's too good to be true. We've been thrown so many cautionary tales about how, "if it's too good to be true, it is." In many cases, that's right. For example, the "get rich quick" schemes out their claim "everyone can be a millionaire" when that's just not the case. Sure, a few, at the very top make it big and party on yachts, but they have stepped on a lot of struggling people (who will always struggle). (Again, I am talking about MLM schemes.)

But, the reality is, that there are ways to build passive income to provide a six-figure (plus) income stream. We don't see these opportunities because we're not exposed to them in business school strategy classes. For example, colleges will not teach you how to find undervalued little services that you can upsell, and hustle to generate income. Many people don't feel like AIS/passive income is a "real" business – you don't have an office – you don't have employees – so, it may not feel real, and you can't see where it can go.

Still, a lot of people are bypassing the old school business model. And you can, too. Find something that sells for a dollar, and re-sell it for five dollars. The traditional internet model involved something like eBay or drop-shipping. Both are legitimate options. But, my approach to AIS takes most of the work out of it, so that once you get things rolling, which takes a tremendous amount of time, everything becomes automated. Therein lies the difference.

Automated Income Stream = Building virtual passive income streams by solving common micro inefficiencies many companies face.

If you are one of the few people still paying for cable, go to the channels that air all the low- budget reality shows. You will notice a common major theme. They illustrate how everyday people can make money buying and selling undervalued items. Whether it's *Pawn Stars*, *Antique Roadshow, Storage Wars, American Packers*, or any of the dozens of home flipping shows, they all focus on how, with a little research and due diligence, you can buy something cheap and resell it at a massive profit. It sounds like a simple concept, but anyone in the industry will tell you the landscape for all of those businesses is saturated and requires a lot of time, capital, and risk.

AIS is a very specific niche type of business concept. We're not out to change the world with some grand idea. We're trying to gain a nice monthly profit based on a very specific need. So, in some ways AIS is a hidden part of the overall business economy. No one is getting interviewed in *Forbes* how they found a service in Fiverr that they are upselling from $1 to $5, and changing the world economy. No. These are "little" things that hold value – that you find – that you recognize as undervalued, and you tweak them to make a profit.

With this book I am going to explain, step-by-step, how you can start a business that uses the same concept of buying cheap and selling high, only with a much higher profit margin and almost no financial risk. I have been employing this formula since I was twenty-one, and while I hit some obstacles early on, the end result paid dividends that have allowed me to travel to 25+ countries, to turn exotic beaches and French cafes into my office, and to become financially independent by my thirtieth birthday.

The insights in this book can help you go from a $30-per-item profit to one of $60. Some of my clients left nine-to-five jobs because they now make $300k+ reselling services off of Fiverr and Upwork, part-time. These are consulting clients who have developed add-on services for their clients. Some are eCom clients who have developed income streams from product groups where clients get specialized advice or gain access to e-courses, webinars, etc.

Pricing

I've talked a little bit about pricing in this book, but let's dive in a little deeper. First, you need to have the understanding that you will not set the price. The customer will. Whatever your customer thinks the product or service is worth is what they'll pay for it. This can be based on their perceived value of the product or service before they're even introduced to the concept of your offer. The value can also be based on what you add to their perception via marketing and selling it to the client – we talk about that in this book, too.

Bottom line, when you think of your product or service, and you're considering the price, you must get into the mind of the consumer. Don't think in percentages (though I always aim for at least a 300% markup), but rather in terms of the value your product or service has for the buyer. Since most of what I talk about regarding AIS is related to service-related products, let's start there.

Let's say you find someone on a freelancer website (like Fiverr or Upwork) who writes killer blog posts, and charges just $10 for a 2,000 word article. You can upsell that to $50. Maybe you have an app developer who puts together great apps that help your clients increase their SEO presence, automatically. They pay you $10 a month for the service. You pay your developer $100 month to maintain and update the app. When you have hundreds of subscribers – well, you can do the math.

I often hear people saying they feel guilty for upselling a service. Don't. Your time is valuable. Chances are that service provider – the blog writer, or the app developer – doesn't have the marketing chops you have, or the connections you'll be developing. They also don't have to deal with the other myriad of costs related to website maintenance, taxes, accounting costs, etc.

These all have to be factored into your calculation around the price – but, remember – the customer sets it. I experiment all the time with price – increasing, mostly. Once a client base is staying on board, and not leaving or cancelling a monthly recurring charge, I know I've priced the service correctly.

Wrapping Your Mind Around AIS

The best way to visualize and understand AIS is that it's not too different from finding something cheap at a yard sale and selling it on eBay for several times more. The only difference is you are doing it with services and software instead of physical goods. I am going to show you the process I use to identify undervalued opportunities, vet them for quality, build a professional brand, and market at a premium rate.

Finding the niche doesn't come from what's in your head. So, finding the service or software that you'll upsell isn't necessarily something you're thinking of right now. We can have all the ideas in the world, but unless there's interest in it, you'll be wasting your time. However, the only way to gauge if there's interest is to put it out there. At some point, you have to be willing to understand and accept whether there is true interest.

In the industry, we say, "Does the dog like the dog food?" Does the consumer, whether or not it's a retail or business consumer, like the service you're providing? If you're getting it out there via killer marketing efforts, but no-one's biting, maybe the service isn't right – or, maybe the price-point is off (see preceding thoughts).

The world has become flat, especially so in the automated technology that doesn't require human interaction. If you know where to look, you can find incredibly undervalued services for which people will easily pay 10-20 times your cost. What makes these services even better is that you don't need to invest in any inventory and you can pay for the service after someone pays you.

While amateur entrepreneurs who have never run a business may gloss over this, it is one of the biggest advantages to the AIS model. You will never have to worry about losing money to inventory going bad, buying too much of a product that is close to expiration so you are forced to sell at a loss, etc. Unlike most businesses, it will be very hard for you to lose money with your AIS as the cost doesn't land until after the sale has been made.

Technology is progressing so rapidly that I think it's impossible to keep up with all the advancements in every industry. Yes, even though you might know the ins and outs of most software/service products in your industry, you probably don't know the first thing about all the technological advances in H.R, Marketing, Payroll, Accounting, etc. This is where AIS comes into play.

A new app or low cost online service could help a company generate millions in extra revenue, or streamline their payroll, or reduce accounting expenses by 80%. Bottom line...there is so much quality, low-cost technology flooding the market that few companies can keep up, especially older, more established companies where the employees who *should* implement these solutions have no incentive to do so.

This is where a savvy AIS'er like you comes in. Imagine you come into a company. You tell the folks about the amazing things you can do to save them several times more than they pay you. Think they might be interested? Why not?

If you want to build long-term passive income you really just need a few core things:

- ➢ a niche that is prime for disruptions,
- ➢ a brand as an Industry Thought Leader in your niche,
- ➢ a low-cost solution with a perceived high-value, and,
- ➢ a low-cost marketing plan to generate new business.

We'll talk about all of these points, and more, within this book. Don't panic. I know it can feel overwhelming, but be assured that I am going to teach you how to and build each of these and get your business running profitable in just a few weeks. It will take some real time and effort, especially at the beginning, but the rewards will be immense.

What's the Catch?

If you're anything like me, you are probably asking, "If building an AIS is so easy and profitable why doesn't everyone do it?" Well, many people are but a lot of them are doing it badly. In fact, the majority of people I meet that are trying to set- up automated income streams are doing it in the least practical way possible. Some great examples of modern day terrible AIS's are selling overpriced essential oils, vitamin shakes, yoga pants, or magical creams and ointments via MLM schemes.

AUTOMATE YOUR INCOME

The difference between what I am going to teach you and the poorly run industries is you are going to create something that has almost no competition, will take a fraction of your time, and is based on providing real value to your clients.

What AIS Is

100% Passive Income: If you need to spend a huge amount of time working on your service, you are doing it wrong. The whole idea of AIS is, essentially, "Set it and forget it."

Freedom: The ability to set your own hours and generate as much or little income as you want. The freedom to take vacations, and earn enough money to finance your life with little to no work involved.

Valuable: The best AIS income opportunities are the ones providing the most value to the customer. The better service you provide, the more revenue you are going to generate. You're not "offering" crap or overpriced products. You are delivering a valuable, needed service to your clients.

What AIS Is Not

MLM/Pyramid Selling: I've mentioned this before, but please do not get sucked into MLM or Direct Selling schemes. When you sign up for one of those, you are *not* a business owner. You are a glorified salesperson and recruiter. With AIS, you are not trying to build your downline or get others under you. In fact, if you find a profitable AIS channel, the *last* thing you want to do is share it with anyone who can duplicate it.

Get Rich Quick Scheme: There is no such thing as easy money! Finding a solid AIS channel takes some trial and error. You will have to test several new offerings and be willing to accept some failures along the way.

How I Created the AIS System

My brain is wired for the AIS system. If I walk out of a dinner party with several AIS ideas, I can't stop thinking about them. While I was working on an AIS project for LinkedIn Marketing, I decided to share ideas on how people could use my AIS concept to generate business for themselves. As I started fleshing out the digital white paper, I realized there was no way I could explain everything in a few PDF pages. I decided to set up a strict writing schedule and devote a few hours every morning to my new obsession. Within a few weeks, this book was born.

I am passionate about this book because I want to give people a guide they can use after we finish our conversation. I love when people that have never started their own company or business hear me explain how easy it is to set up a business destined to double their yearly salaries. I believe most people have the ability to do great things if they have a solid blueprint.

Why Everyone Should Put Their Incomes on Autopilot

There is an old saying that people should work *on* their business and not *in* it. Some people do not understand the difference. They have never owned an enterprise, so they completely underestimate how hard scaling one is. I've met more entrepreneurs than most and I can honestly say, most don't have any clue what they are doing when it comes to building their businesses and are frantically trying to figure it out. You have it right when you finally dial in the model and it runs even if you aren't in the equation. When you are looking to build an AIS model, you should have the same goal – a 100% automated model that runs independent of your involvement.

So, are AIS's really just starting a business? I guess, technically, when you build an AIS you are starting a business, but there are huge differences between the two.

Here are just a few of the reasons why I prefer AIS over starting a "traditional" business or start-up:

No Employees: Most businesses rely on employees to scale and grow. Even the smallest businesses typically have a few employees involved. I think employees throw a major variable of uncertainty into the formula, which is the #1 reason why I prefer AIS over launching a new, traditional business.

Recurring Revenue: If you set up your AIS properly, you should be able to build long-term, recurring revenue on a monthly basis even if you do nothing. While there are some business models that pay you long residuals for each sale, they are hard to come by and are typically only in industries with high barriers to entry. (You aren't starting your own cable or cell phone company.) Planning is simplified. If you are netting $20,000 each month from an AIS service and you want to increase by 5%, you know you need to add "x" number of clients. So, you can plan and market (and spend) accordingly.

Automated Work: Ideally, you want your work performed by a robot or software. Sometimes you will need to outsource a service but you do so at a fraction of the client's cost. In most cases, you do not want to touch the AIS – you just want the income to roll in every month.

Creating Your Own Work Schedule: AIS is all about building a system and then sitting back and collecting the monthly earnings.

Scalability: Once you learn the process, you can set up dozens of channels independently that will create revenue for years.

The Good, The Bad, and The Ugly

Before we get into the specifics, you need to understand the basic concepts on what makes a good AIS opportunity and what will utterly waste your time.

Non-competitive Niche Verticals: When you begin on your path to automating your income, it's important to find some easier, less-competitive industries. For example, you could try to negotiate some type of referral commission off getting a company to switch insurance providers. Chances are, however, the company gets hit by insurance agents daily, so you won't be able to cut through the noise. Note: Sales is one of the best niches in AIS because most companies have no issue paying for sales.

Services that are easily automated: If you want to make passive income, choose a process that can be almost 100%

automated. Luckily, technology is adding more and more ways to automate even the most minute tasks.

Good: Hire a full-time outsourced freelancer. This is the most common option, and also the most frustrating. This is the classic 40 hour work-week model where you outsource parts of your job or a service to someone willing to work for a lower fee.

Better: Outsource the entire service to a company that will complete it from start to finish. For example, you have a company that is great at making short videos for social media content. You have the clients email you their thoughts and creative ideas and you send everything to the outsource company.

Best: A service that can be fully automated through software. For instance, you set up a custom widget tied into QuickBooks and it runs automatically for a client.

Note: I would highly recommend starting a service that isn't a one-off; try to find a service with monthly recurring income. With a one-off service, you'll be constantly scrambling to get new customers. The exception to this would be a one-off requiring "refills," like the Breathalyzer Keychain.

To review:

Bad AIS Model: "I will write and publish a new blog post for $50!"

Good AIS Model: "I will write and publish a new blog post every week for $199 a month!"

When I was twenty, I worked with Indian developers who helped me put together a backlink program I could sell to my clients for between $1.99 and $2.99 a month. It helped the clients increase visibility and credibility in their field. With my marketing and sales efforts, I had hundreds of clients paying for the service every month. My cost was between $7 and $15 a month. My developers put the algorithms together for the clients. We eventually developed a million+ dollar business.

In 2014, when algorithms changed on Google, it all came crashing down. So, with the same team, and some new team members, we adapted to other marketing techniques for our existing clients. We attracted new clients with services like writing blog posts, content marketing, and so-on. These were basic pay-per-click management models where my costs were about $20 a month. I charged $400 to overlook and build the systems.

I made this my first AIS for a couple of reasons. It was great timing. I'd made mistakes, learned a lot, and recognized the opportunity as something I could handle. I had also found the right partner in my Indian counterpart. And, it was a great service to provide. One of the cool things about backlinks is the client can't see them – they require no client input.

When I was first getting started, I was dealing with web design. In that type of work, you move throughout the process from initial outlines – to drafts – to adding images and text boxes. The client has 100% control you're your work and can see everything you do – good or bad. The same holds true for content writing. They read the text. If they do not like the "voice" or the message, they toss it back and you rewrite. The back and forth seems unending. The client is never happy – does not want to pay for stuff you do over because he/she thinks you should have gotten it right the first time.

With backlinks, clients had no idea what we were doing. All they saw were the results – the rankings. No review – no, "Let's try this" – no, "I don't like the way that sounds." We did what we needed to do and gave the client the results they were looking and paying for.

Another great feature of backlinks: clients *had* to continue on a monthly basis if they wanted to grow. The goal post was not a month out – it was one, two, three years away. We were always looking to move up in the rankings. All the goals were long-term and required a regular and recurring commitment to drive rankings every upward. When done right, clients will stay with you for a decade or more.

Every single business and business owner needs backlinks to improve their rankings. The more backlinks, the higher the rating. Every business wants to build its visibility and credibility on search engines, so every single business owner you meet is a potential client.

When we talk about niches related to AIS, I don't mean client niches as much as I mean service niches. Instead of trying to build and provide a software program that is the be-all and end-all for a business, that "does everything," look for a minutely niched service that everyone needs – even if they don't know it – yet.

Characteristics of Bad AIS Models

Let's start with what *doesn't* work. As you're thinking about what type of AIS business you want to start, rule out these flops:

"Small Company" Clients: Smaller businesses are typically much more money conscious and less likely to pay a premium for a service even if it's amazing. The budgets just aren't there, typically, for them to invest in beneficial services. In addition, you have to recruit ten small companies to achieve the income potential from one larger client.

MLM Products: I know – I beat this to death. But before I get bombarded with negative reviews and emails – I get it, your boss's high school friend, Tom, who drives a new Corvette, makes hundreds of thousands a year selling some type of new-age groundbreaking supplement. While I'm happy for Tom, the fact is that most people lose a massive amount of money in MLM participation, so I suggest avoiding them like the plague.

Regulated Businesses: Here was another factor in the Breathalyzer Keychain failure. Whenever you enter a business that is highly regulated, you have to have *a lot* of capital to fight through any problems. Best to avoid anything burdened with city, state, or – gasp – federal regulations. Perform your due diligence – put in the research time. If you find that your potential niche is highly regulated, walk away and find something that isn't watched so tightly by folks in out-of-date suits.

No Clear Objective: Before you start any AIS, clearly define the terms. Lay out (in writing) what you will be doing – and what you won't. From my experience, clients are quick to agree to things in the beginning but will become more needy over time. If a client wants a higher level of service or more work, be direct and say, "That wasn't in the contract, but I can do that for X% more."

Client is involved in the process: If your service requires client approval or sign-offs, it will typically fail in the first few weeks. I do not trust anyone else to meet a timetable. The last thing I want to do is spend my week reminding them to do their job, so I can do mine.

Thin Margins: Some of my most profitable AIS programs also have the thinnest margins, but it took me over a decade to dial them in, and even then the risk was high. I would not offer a service that doesn't make at least 3X your investment.

Pro tip: Your time is valuable. Remember to factor it you're your equation.

Reflection

Why do you want to put your income on autopilot?

_____
_____
_____
_____

What are you currently doing that's preventing it from happening? What are you doing that's promoting it?

_____
_____
_____
_____

What are some new ways you can build passive income?

_____
_____
_____
_____

"Content marketing is more than a buzzword. It is the hottest trend in marketing because it is the biggest gap between what buyers want and brands produce."

Michael Brenner

Chapter 3

Developing Your Stream

"Fill the void in the market!" – one of the most important steps in developing a profitable AIS stream. Some folks accomplish the goal in a few days – others take months. You've probably run across amazing AIS opportunities every day without recognizing them.

So, how can you train your brain to recognize AIS opportunities?

Identifying and Vetting AIS Service Opportunities

Listen to people complaining about bottlenecks. Ask people what frustrates them with their job. "What is your company doing wrong, but can't or won't fix?" "What simple thing would make your job much easier?" If someone mentions the quality of sales leads are terrible, you can suggest a digital marketing funnel to help them prospect. If they say the website looks like it was put together by a three-year-old kid, recommend a new CMS upgrade.

If you are seen as an "expert" in the field of streamlining things in your industry, you'll quickly become a go-to person. One way you solidify your reputation is by staying current with new technologies in your industry. Everything tech changes almost daily. Last year' s "hot info" may be worthless today. (You do not want an 8-track mentality or knowledge in a "streaming world.") Know what was available yesterday, what's in the pipeline for the next few months, and where things are trending for the next year and beyond. There are no shortcuts to acquiring this knowledge. Make time for research even if just for a few minutes each day.

Getting On Top – and Staying There

You never know when you are going to run across a prospect, so always have a business card handy. I usually tell people to give me a call, so I can give them some type of free advice on whatever they are trying to do. Helping someone (for free) keeps you on the front of the stove. You want ways to offer value? Try variations of these:

Marketing: "I've marketed a number of companies in that industry. Call me next week and I can tell you what worked for them."

Web/Graphic Design: "I have a really good design I did with another client who never finished the project; I think it could work for your company. Let's hop on a call next week."

Content Writing: "I think the reason so many people in your industry fail is they aren't putting themselves in the buyer's shoes. I've developed a few quick and easy hacks I think would work for your industry. What time works for you next week?"

Search Engine Optimization: "I can run a few quick audits on your website to make sure no one is using a black hat SEO against you. It's way more common than you think. Just give me the URL and I'll take a look for you."

Video Production: "I found a strategy that uses short videos to dominate the Facebook and Instagram algorithms. I bet they would work well for your industry. I'll walk you through how it works on a call next week."

Best Industries For Building an AIS

Here's a little known secret. The best industries to strike for building an effective and highly profitable AIS are not what you think. Older industries that haven't embraced technology advances, like manufacturing, finance, construction, skilled trades (HVAC, plumbing, electrical), government, and retail brick and mortar, are your best targets. Why? Often times these businesses are "set in their ways" and don't follow technological advancements that might greatly automate their industry. Even after you show them the technology, they may not want to be bothered and will pay you to handle everything.

Don't Fall in Love With Your First AIS

My first AIS was a disaster. I was trying to sell "backlinks" to businesses to get their websites to rank higher in search engine results. It all started when I met someone in India who had created a way to trick the search engines by artificially inflating the number of links to their website. It had worked great for another place where I worked, so he and I cobbled together an unofficial partnership. I resold to local businesses.

I knocked on doors as I tried to sell a service guaranteed to put a business in the coveted #1 search engine spot (Google and Bing) for their local industry. No one bit! In hindsight, I see exactly why it failed and what I could have done differently, but at twenty-one years old (and desperate to move out of my parents' house), I cut too many corners.

I managed to stay profitable for a while by building add-ons and other services to my client base. But, when the Google Penguin update hit the search engine, it eliminated backlinks as a ranking tool. With one push of a button, Google wiped out my entire service – one that had been doing millions a year for over a decade.

Gulp!

Here's the lesson: if I had fallen in love with that first AIS – backlinks – I wouldn't have seen the other services I could offer to help clients reach their ultimate goal – increased revenue. *That* was the service I was selling – not the specific backlink – ways to increase traffic and visibility intended to result in more money for my clients.

When I discuss AIS models with people, they always have a lot of ideas. I want to fuel their passion. I need to see *the entire forest* (all the possibilities) not just *an individual tree* (one AIS concept). I learned to test the waters with several different routes before committing to anything specific. In the startup world we refer to this as an MVP (Minimal Viable Product); the idea is to get a quick but stable version out for testing.

Why An AIS Fails

Just because *you* think a product or service is amazing does not mean the customer will love it. So, what are the top reasons for failure with an AIS?

The service is too complicated: While the concept is common-sense in your mind, a company may have a hard time understanding the benefits it will receive. You must make the pitch super simple to understand. Prepare a one-pager designed to answer all the top questions.

Not Cost Effective: If you have a service that will save a company $500 a month but costs $250 a month, you will have a hard time selling it. For a company to purchase a service, the juice has to be worth the squeeze.

Lack of Hype: Most people who are not in the marketing world don't realize how much they are being manipulated to purchase a product or service. "Market funnels" drag consumers towards a sale. When you are making your pitch, grab everyone's attention with "the big promise." Subtlety does nothing for you – explain how your service will *change someone's life..*

Too Time Consuming: Make sure the AIS requires the absolute minimum investment of time from the company. One of the fastest ways to get rejected is for clients to think they are going to have to spend a massive amount of time on the system. For example, implementing a software system that includes a huge learning curve for staff and may disrupt operations for several days or weeks when initially integrated will not get anyone excited.

eCom Based AIS Opportunities

I am not a fan of an eCom AIS because it requires more hands-on work than the other models. Unless you go 100% into drop shipping, you will bog down with logistics and customer service nightmares. Amazon is monopolizing eCom. I know people who have lost everything. They had multimillion dollar businesses – Amazon backdoored them and negotiated with the owner of their product provider. My colleagues had to shut their doors and got stuck with tons of inventory.

When I got involved with eCom in manufacturing my own products, I completely underestimated how much was involved, from hiring employees to putting things together, shipping products, dealing with returns, and so on. I don't care how good you are, you can't build a sustainable company if you try to do it all by yourself. The time and energy (and money) required to enter an eCom enterprise is not worth it, in my view.

Unless you have a drop shipper with a fully automated processes (few and far between), you must deal with lost shipments and broken, defective, or damaged merchandise. Even with my initial success in eCom product selling, I am not a fan.

A side note: most drop shipping comes out of China. In my experience, many manufacturers in China will burn you. There is no loyalty. If they know there's another person in line who wants the same product you're offering, they will build a cheap knockoff of your product and totally undercut you. Or, they'll just send you something completely different from what you ordered. Unless you (or your representative) stands in the factory, you have a real chance of getting worked.

One time, a factory sent an order of a cheap knock-off of the original product – not something I could accept. I called the company. Guess what? They were out of business. As smart as I think I am, I've gotten burned for hundreds of thousands of dollars by manufacturers in China through multiple scams and drop shipping schemes. If you are determined to go ahead, proceed with extreme caution, and consider working with a professional who has experience with managing Chinese manufacturing processes.

If you do go with drop shipping, use U.S. based sources like MarketPlace Valet. They will charge you 15 to 20 percent higher on the wholesale end, but you'll save in headaches and avoid potential disasters.

MarketPlace Valet helps brands greatly simplify their process of selling on multiple online marketplaces like eBay and Amazon. They handle the entire process from beginning to end. Their listing management and fulfillment systems allow you to focus on brand building and development while they do the selling, shipping and other services. This type of service is unbeatable if you're going to consider eCom sales as they tend to put the "A" in "AIS."

With that said, I have had a few successes in the vertical. I shot a video in my backyard for one project. The video went viral (55k likes, 8,500 comments, 12M views). I pulled in six figures solely from an ad that took less than an hour to shoot. Here's the link: https://www.facebook.com/watch/?v=1114292821965492

If you owned an iPhone in 2016 and were on Facebook, chances are you saw me at least a few times on your news feed. I made a simple product with great margins, and once I dialed in the ad campaign, we ramped up sales to over $230,000 in the first 30 days. We exceeded $2,000,000 in the first year. Here's how I did it.

AUTOMATE YOUR INCOME

It all started when I met a smart, ambitious, guy who hit me up for a meeting to discuss a business idea about getting into the expanding wood promotional product space. I knew nothing about the vertical but I have always bet on people, not products, so I gave it a shot.

Early on we hit snags like any business, but we quickly established a good rhythm and found an opening in the market with massive potential. As many of you recall, the news at the time overflowed with headlines about Apple's battery issues. Updates sucked power out of older phones, so battery cases became more of a necessity than a luxury. There was no way I was going to open an electronics business company and compete in the technology space; however, I did see an angle that might work...sticking wood veneer on poorly marketed, existing battery cases.

The industry was still pretty small at the time. The lack of competition meant most of the bigger companies in the space weren't spending a lot on R&D. We took it upon ourselves to test every battery case we could from other countries where competition was stiffer. Once we selected the perfect, cheap shiny plastic cover, we covered it with processed wood.

Minimal resources raised the value of the product substantially. The genius of AIS.

After a few weeks of testing we launched more and more products and enjoyed instant success on social media.

Videos I'd shot in the back of my office building were getting tens of millions of views and tens of thousands of comments. We passed several million dollars in sales in the first year.

At the end of the day, however, I realized it was too much hands-on work for me. In addition, Chinese manufacturers started undercutting us and our profits sank. I looked for something easier and less time dependent.

We listed the company, got acquired, and teamed up on a much more profitable venture.

Tips for Building an eCom AIS

Keep it Simple: Find something that can be quickly and cheaply manufactured with minimal out-of-pocket investment. Avoid making or developing your own product from scratch.

Don't Handle Shipping: I cannot stress enough that you should stay *far away as possible* from shipping your own products. The learning curve as you scale is massive. You have to deal with every imaginable problem – returns, incorrect addresses, tracking, warehousing, and all the rest. Remember, most firms involved in shipping devote entire departments to those issues. You can always dropship products or use a company like MarketPlace Valet, someone who can and will handle 100% of the logistics for you.

Service Based Opportunities: Before I write about the different service industries I like, let me say you don't need to know anything about an industry to sell it. Yes, it helps if you know all the industry specific acronyms and jargon; it's by no means essential. While many of my AIS funnels were marketing related, I focused there because I could cross/upsell to the same person and increase my lifetime value of the customer (this is known as LTV in the industry).

I always recommend starting within your own industry. If you encounter trouble finding a good solution, research highly-rated/cheap services on freelance and job sites like freelancer.com, Upwork, and Fiverr. Think how you can re-package and sell a given service for a premium. Another way of expanding your AIS offer is to combine two services and offer it into one. Here are some services I have combined in the past:

- Email Content Writing + Email Promotion
- Website Design + Search Engine Optimization
- Press Release Writing + PR Distribution
- Lead Generation + Sales Funnel Implementation
- Logo Design + Animated 3D Logos
- Facebook Ads + Chatbot Implementation

I go to Fiverr, or Upwork (or some other freelancing platform) and order the service myself. I check out the quality – I want to ensure I am getting what I ordered. I find the opportunities, then package them and wrap them in a bow, so I can sell them at a much higher price tag. The idea is to find something no one else is doing – or to make something more in-tune with today's market and the demands of today's technology consumers.

Email Trickling

There is available software that does "email trickling." You can sign up for a Gmail account, use this software, and it will send two dozen, customized emails per day. It's not spam, because it's only sending a few dozen emails a day. All the software needs is a downloaded list of target names and websites. The program generates very customized emails and delivers them.

A friend of mine uses trickling software. He pays $100 a month for unlimited accounts, and sets his clients up with a simple Gmail account. The customers pay him $99-$299 a month (depending on the account size) for lead prospecting. He can typically get his client's 5 to 10 solid leads per week at practically no cost. The software does everything for him. To repeat, he sets and forgets. He's pulling in six-figures, part-time, without any management worries (as long as there are no software glitches).

Another friend, Adam Palm (www.upworksavedmylife), built a seven-figure business by putting together different pieces of software and building the ideal funnel together for people trying to sell an e-course, virtual product, or system. His isn't completely automated, as he has to put time into it, but he charges anywhere from $500-$600 an hour, and has automated upsell services on the back-end he uses to create loyal clients.

Go on Fiverr and look at the top-reviewed services. Most of the people looking for services on Fiverr are smaller, start-up operations. Find a way to take a service, upgrade it, and add or combine services to pitch it to a mid-size company.

What are a few of the services you might like to tap?

Marketing: Almost every business needs help marketing, and few understand even the first steps on how to do it correctly. The way technology is changing, it's difficult for those of us who live and breathe in the industry to stay current.

Sales: One of the easiest ways to land your first AIS is to get paid on the sales you generate for a company. Sounds difficult, but find the right business and you will be golden.

Accounting: Many companies are in the dark ages when it comes to bookkeeping. I have seen people charge massive premiums for integrating basic accounting features into their clients' QuickBooks.

Adding Value to Your AIS

To build a successful AIS, you must provide some value to the service or product you are reselling. Sometimes this can be as easy as additional consulting or reporting, but I encourage you to as much value as you can while keeping everything streamlined and automatic.

Here are some simple offers you can extend to appeal to your customers:

Free Memberships: People love being part of a group and many groups charge a membership fee. You can create a private community that all current customers can access for free as long as they are a client.

Discounts & Promos: Ever wonder why so many credit cards offer discounts and coupons when you sign up for a new account? The card's high perceived value does not cost the company anything. In fact, many of the vendors (of the free items) pay a commission to the card company on top of the discount they give to the new customers.

Free Publications: Everyone loves publicity. Offer free monthly interviews on your social media profiles or on a free content platform like Medium.com. What's great about this value add is – it costs nothing.

Sell Results!

Value also means providing good service. Are you giving your clients what you promise them? Can you *demonstrate your value* with real and live data? For example, if you are promising to increase email open rates by "xx" percent, can you show "Before" and "After" stats? Value comes from the end-result, not the services you're selling. I wasn't selling backlinks; I was selling how to increase revenue organically through search engine optimization.

If you can really sell and show results, people will throw money at you. They won't care how much it costs. They'll know your service saves time and money. With those types of clients, you can set benchmarks, and say, "If I can deliver 'xx' this month, would you be willing to spend '$yy' extra next month, and thereafter, to keep the momentum going?" Deliver results and you will have exceptionally loyal clients who will grow with you.

Reflection

What void in the market can you fill?

_____
_____
_____
_____

In what ways does your customer view your product/service differently from the way you see it?

_____
_____
_____
_____

What changes about your product/service need the most attention?

_____
_____
_____
_____

"Social media is about the people. Not about your business. Provide for the people and the people will provide for you."

Matt Goulart

Chapter 4

Starting Your Journey

Before you make your first sale, set up a website that sums up your service and gives the visitor a little backstory. A website establishes instant credibility and allows you to brag (humbly) about your accomplishments and expertise. As your company grows, you will start getting referral and search traffic at no cost – basically free sales. Luckily, there are a ton of low-cost website builder tools at your disposal – pick out what you need. Here are a few of my favorites from most to least.

Shopify: To me, Shopify has everything a novice needs to create a beautiful, well-performing website quickly and easily. I have built several Shopify sites and have never encountered any type of issue. The apps are all plug-and-play throughout the platform, the support is awesome, and the merchant account is tied right in. Start on this platform if you are looking for a plug-and-play solution.

SquareSpace: SquareSpace has come a long way over the years and is my #1 pick for anyone looking to build a website on a budget. It's search engine friendly, has decent plugins, and the learning curve isn't terrible. There are some big reputable websites being built on SquareSpace such as Joe Rogan.

Wix: I've never been a massive fan of Wix, but some people swear it's the easiest to use. The big downside to Wix is that it severely limits what you can do on the basic platform. If you are very uncomfortable with tech, this might be a good option, but I would at least try some of the more robust platforms before committing to Wix.

WordPress: WordPress is by far the most customizable platform, but it is also the most advanced, so it can be difficult to master. I've seen many amateurs waste months, even years, of their lives trying to customize a WordPress site.

On your website, you are not just selling something. If you are, you will scare many potential clients away. These days, people are savvier online than ever before, and they are looking for quality content. If you provide quality information on your website and on your social media accounts – free – people will line up to become your clients.

Becoming an Industry Thought Leader

If you want people to buy from you, they must believe you have something worthwhile to say. The easiest way to build trust is to establish yourself as a thought leader in your industry. Becoming a respected thought leader doesn't happen overnight, but if you follow the steps below, you can build a great and growing foundation.

Register All Your Social Media Handles

The first step in becoming a thought leader is to register all your social media handles, even if you don't plan on using them.

While you may not use all the platforms now, you may start using them as your business grows and your business becomes your primary income source.

There are many free/cheap pieces of software that allow you to post across all social platforms at the same time.

Search engines use social media profile activity to determine where to rank sites in their results. By having active profiles on all the platforms, you have a better chance to generate free, organic traffic to your website. Once your business grows, you may want to start running ads to hit a wider audience. The more active profiles you have, the more you can split test ads across different platforms to test what platforms give your unique service the best ROI. Don't let ads scare you! Here are a few easy ways to split test ads.

- If you build a site on Shopify, you can use one of several apps that plug right into the CMS. I have had good luck with Neat A/B Testing.
- You can try a simple landing page builder. Most have the split test option built into the software. I like Instapage and Lead pages.
- If you are tech savvy and build in WordPress there are many free and paid plugins that have a massive number of options. I use Thrive Optimize (paid) and Google Optimizer (free).

Post Daily, Quality Content

As mentioned before, the more quality content you post, the more your following will be built, organically. After some time, and with enough quality content on your site, you can start running ads to hit a wider audience. But, stretch out the use of organic (aka free) exposure as much as you can.

Share Your Expertise

Stay on top of your industry, so that your expertise shines through. Share that expertise via blog posts and quality content. There are no shortcuts to becoming an industry leader. You have to know your stuff. The minute you start "faking" it, people will run away from you in droves. Those people are potential clients. So, you need to be knowledgeable, and seen as someone who can be helpful for those who are not savvy in your industry. Take time, every day, to find out new information about your industry. Write about it, and share that information. If you're one of the first to "share the love," you'll be seen as a leader, because you are.

Go Past Your Website

Write opinion pieces and share with industry related magazines, journals, websites and social media accounts. Industry-related sites are always looking for quality content – opinions, reviews and information. As long as you're not actively "selling," your input will be extremely welcome.

Reach Out

Reach out to industry related podcasts. At first, you may contact thirty of them, but only be asked for one interview. That's great. Next time two will want to talk to you. Don't stop. Soon, you'll be a go-to and higher quality podcasts and news sources will seek you out.

Repeat steps 2 through 5: Nothing happens overnight. It may be months or years before you see substantial progress. But, trust me, the time you put in will be worth it. In just a few years, you can be seen as an industry leader, someone people think of when topics come up related to your field. You can't "buy" your way to status – ads can help down the line after you have some content, articles and interviews under your belt. But, your expertise, if you market it correctly, will be tapped into, resulting in a trust factor that will automatically lead to sales and success.

Building a Strong Personal Brand

Many people fail because they don't understand the importance of building a personal brand. With the AIS streams, it's much more important to have a personal brand than a corporate one (though if you are going to build several AIS's it makes sense to build at least a small brand around each).

I started building my own personal brand by getting on the local news, becoming involved in local charities and organizations, joining for-profit and nonprofit boards, and just getting involved in the community. On a national level, participation with groups like the YEC really pushed my visibility upward, as (through their networks) I had articles published in national and international magazines. Within networks like YEC, you have the opportunity to help someone else make money, so your name spreads, and you build a reputation, and brand, quickly.

Social networking is, by far, the best and worst thing that can happen to you as you're building a personal brand. You can either get your name demolished in every ad, with people calling you a fake or a phony (which I see all the time). But, if people like you, they will become your advocates and they'll turn those negative comments into positives.

Give people real advice, do not bullshit them, make sure that they are happy, give them a full refund if they are dissatisfied (even if the fault is on their end). All those actions build a great brand. Success is not just about marketing yourself; it's about having a truly reliable, honest and reputable brand and service that you provide to your clients. People will trust you and everything you do down the road.

The first step to building your brand is reflecting inward and identifying what personality type you have. While most people are a blend of several personality types, you usually display one prominent type. How you build depends largely on your personality type.

Personality Types

Personality type: The Salesperson

Overview: A salesperson is someone who understands how to communicate and build a relationship with a potential client, gently "pushing" them towards the sale.

Examples of successful salespeople archetypes: Gary Vaynerchuck, Tony Robbins, etc.

How a Salesperson builds a personal brand
Salespeople are naturally comfortable talking directly with potential clients, so they should build their brand around their ability to inspire confidence and build trust.
Record as much content as possible. Filming yourself is a great way to stay on the "top of the mind" – drop feed your sales message to potential clients. Participate in as many live interviews as possible. Let your charisma shine – give people a chance to know you.

Personality Type: The Techie

Overview: The Techie is someone who isn't afraid of using new technology and has a natural passion to understand and dissect new social platforms, website CRMs, and plug ins.

Examples of successful Techies: Bill Gates, Steve Jobs

How Techies build a personal brand

The main goal for techies in building a personal brand is to spotlight their ability to understand complex technologies that many of their potential clients cannot, and to explain the technologies in an easy-to-understand way.

Product Demos are a great way to communicate with your audience without having to be in front of a camera. You can pre-record demos and edit them for hours before ever publishing live. With demos, you can break down the "how & why" of your product without hiding behind technical jargon. White papers allow you to push a sale without ever picking up a phone or driving to a coffee shop. A well-constructed white paper answers every objection anyone has and completes 99% of the sale.

Personal Type: The Connector

Overview: The Connector is a social butterfly. Building relationships comes naturally. Connectors usually have a large network of friends and acquaintances and are active on several social media accounts.

Examples of Successful Connectors: Benjamin Franklin (he may not have had social media, but there is no denying his power as a connector), Bill Gates (not just a techie, but a master at creating software building networks), Donald Trump (love him or hate him, he had constructed a massive empire of connections), the Kardashians ('nuf said).

How Connectors build a personal brand

The key to developing your connector brand is to get out there. Build relationships and foster collaboration. Someone who connects can build their personal brand by:

- Joining local and national groups
- Becoming involved and connect with others in their fields
- Writing articles for group magazines or publications
- Being a visible face within the group(s).

Connect people in your industry. Let's say you want to bring two services together. Start a conversation with two different industry leaders about how to bring their services together. You'll be seen as someone who gets things done by collaborative work with others.

Regardless of your personality profile, building your personal brand is critical to getting your name and good reputation into the public consciousness. In the beginning, you'll have to work hard to get your ideas and information out there. As you become more well-known in the field or industry, your work will be on maintaining and improving (always there's room for improvement) your image and personal brand.

Don't dismiss the importance of developing a powerful and positive personal brand. People who know, like, and trust you – and you are the face of your company and in many ways, you are the company – will buy from you, over and over again. That is the power of developing a positive personal brand. If you get mired down in the branding, at the cost of not paying attention enough to the service and quality of the customer experience you provide, people will very quickly look for someone else. A good service and a good brand will sell themselves.

As important as building a positive, powerful personal brand is, building it up should take no more than 10% of your time. Spend the other 90% of your time improving your services and on finding and testing new ones. You are *constantly* marketing what you have and *always* working to improve your AIS.

Reflection

What's your personality type? What part of your business do you specialize the most in?

_____
_____
_____
_____

How much of you is focused on your personal brand? In relation, how much of you is focused on improving your AIS?

_____
_____
_____
_____

How can you improve your AIS right now?

_____
_____
_____
_____

"Marketing is telling the world you're a rock star. Content marketing is showing the world you are one."

Robert Rose

Chapter 5

Building Authority in a Niche

Let's take some time to talk about building authority in a niche market. How do you get people to recognize you are an absolute expert in a specific area? You've seen people like this; you may even follow them on Instagram. They are the people you admire. When they tell you something, you believe it. You care about how they think.

And you want to be like them – you want to occupy a similar space.

There are no fast tracks or short cuts to get to the top, but I will give you some ideas to make the process more efficient and effective. My tips won't make you a Tony Robbins or Grant Cardone, but you will have a niche following based on your audience's perception of you as a reliable resource and expert in the field. Remember, you're not necessarily trying to appeal to the masses – instead, you're trying to tap into your niche audience and gain footing in your area.

Here are some thoughts as you explore the notion of building authority. Remember, you don't have to do all of these at the same time. Take one at a time and increase your efforts slowly and steadily until you are creating the type of following that you're looking for:

Interviewing Subject Matter Experts

A simple way to build credibility as an authority is to interview subject matter experts in your niche. If you are having trouble finding subject matter experts, interview high level execs in other industries about your niche. If your niche is building custom 3D logos and animations, you can interview CEOs on the importance of having a strong brand.

Getting Unlimited Interviews – Building a Media Portal

In the age of technology, it's laughably easy for anyone to get interviews with CEOs, CMOs, or even celebrities with no money out of pocket. Basically, everyone wants to be recognized for their accomplishments and are looking for places to "humble brag." Generating hundreds of interview requests is as easy as building a free media portal and bulk messaging PR companies.

Step 1: You want a portal where you can showcase your talent. The best method is to build your own website or create a "magazine" on a free content site such as Medium.com.

Step 2: Once the portal is built, conduct a few interviews with friends or family, so the site doesn't look empty. Once you have five live interviews, start messaging PR companies. Tell them you would like to interview some of their clients on a specific topic. PR companies are very motivated to connect you with their clients because they get paid per article regardless of the size. You can find interviews by posting to PR Facebook pages – you'd be surprised how many contacts you can get this way.

Step 3: A quick way to bang out interviews is to send pre-written questions in an interview format. This allows you to upload an interview to the site after just a few minutes of proofreading. However, if you want to squeeze more out of each interview, I highly recommend video interviews using a software like Zoom.

Video Interview Tips:

Tip 1: Ask exciting questions. You want people to be interested in the answers. Here are a few suggestions.

- What was the biggest mistake you made in business?
- Looking back, what is your #1 regret in business?
- What is something most people outside your industry don't know about it?

Tip 2: Cutting through the noise and getting someone's attention is tough, so make sure you give your clips exciting headlines that will make people want to stop scrolling and watch. For example:

- Veteran Entrepreneur Reveals #1 Issue With Privatizing Healthcare
- Digital Marketer Drops a Bomb About Google AdWords
- Banking CEO Fires Back at Newest Trump Tweet

Tip 3: Always upload video content directly to the social media platform. Social platforms don't link to another platform and will penalize you heavily. Don't be lazy. Instead of cutting and pasting a YouTube link on Facebook, take the time to upload the clip.

Tip 4: Take any interview you've given and cut it into short sections. No one is going to watch you talk for thirty minutes. But, if you subdivide the piece into juicy, 20-second snippets, people will hang on every word. You can then use those clips as retargeting ads, social media content, your own online magazine (through platforms like medium.com), on your blog posts, in emails, and much more. People love watching videos, and good ones will set you apart from someone who is writing blogs with just words and a few pretty pictures.

Getting Awards & Accolades

A quick way to build brand authority is to display whatever awards and accolades you've accumulated over the years. Here are some ways to achieve recognition.

Engage With Groups Where Your Clients Hang Out: If you want to be recognized for your intelligence by your peers, sometimes you have to earn it one-by-one instead of shouting, "I'm a genius" from the rooftops. I have made some of the best partnerships and referral partners from groups where I am active. I make sure I'm involved, giving back, and staying in everyone's good graces. From there, your visibility shoots up.

Joining a group gives you the ability to answer questions and to establish that you know what you are talking about. Every question you answer, or every intelligent discussion you start, builds a little more credibility to your name and makes you more of an influencer in your industry. You can also fast track your growth by supporting and contributing to charities. (This carries the double benefit of improving your community.) In one week, I raised enough money for a local charity to be listed in the "Top 50 Community Leaders" in my mid-sized city.

Use Humor: I can't stress this enough – the quickest way to become memorable is to make someone chuckle at a meme, video, or comic. Making memes comes naturally for me, so I typically create them myself on the fly. If you feel really creative, check out the Meme economy. It's a fictional stock market where people "invest" in what memes will take off. These concepts can usually be edited for almost any purpose.

I follow several meme directories – ones I can edit to apply to my industry. For example, follow nursing meme Facebook pages and change "the nurse" content to your own industry.

Be Helpful: The more helpful you are in a group, the more respect you will build. If you only post when you are trying to sell something, you will quickly be branded as someone to avoid. Give as much in-depth help as you can, even if you are not directly benefiting from it. You will be able to cash in on this goodwill at some point, though it may be indirectly.

Give Away Free Stuff: If I have an opportunity to give something away for free, I find it almost always results in instant unexplained sales. A quick, easy way to get people excited is to give something away. You could offer five free copies of your digital book for honest feedback, an interview on your blog or content portal or, my personal favorite, a video screenshare on how you figured out something interesting to the group.

Once you earn an award or accolade, don't be afraid to show it off. Make it part of your personal brand. Include it on a website, in your marketing material. Your awards and accolades are bricks you use to build your personal brand – one at a time.

Don't forget about your services and the product that you provide. Your personal brand is critical to growing your business and creating loyal followers who will pay you for your services. But, at the top of your priorities is establishing a brand by building your services, exploring new options and add-ons, and testing services for which your clients will willingly pay.

Reflection

In what ways can you improve your personal brand in groups?

_____
_____
_____
_____

What awards and accomplishments do you wish to gain?

_____
_____
_____
_____

What awards and accomplishments have you already gained? How can you use them as a marketing tool?

_____
_____
_____
_____

"Content is king, but engagement is queen, and the lady rules the house!"

Mari Smith

Chapter 6

Leveraging Your Followers

A large part of my process involves building a tribe around your brand. It's hard to get someone to buy from you until they really feel they know you, so it's important to stay in front of your followers and continually stay top-of-mind when they think about your industry. Fortune 500 companies spend a significant amount of revenue on billboards, banners, and TV ads to reinforce their brand over and over until it finally sinks in.

We all know it is infinitely easier to keep customers, and to turn them into a super-customer, than to get a new one. According to SmallBizTrends:

"Acquiring a new customer can cost five times more than retaining an existing customer. Increasing customer retention by 5% can increase profits from 25-95%. The success rate of selling to a customer you already have is 60-70%, while the success rate of selling to a new customer is 5-20%."

Building loyalty is the secret to any successful business, but is especially critical when it comes to leveraging your followers in an AIS business. In today's business environment, your social media presence is everything. You can't just throw things out there anymore – today's consumer is savvier than ever. You must provide value and build trust to expand your tribe and to create the leverage that gives back to you – over and over and over again.

If you're reading this book, I'm pretty sure you're not running a Fortune 500 business – and neither am I. So, what are some ways to leverage your tribe into revenue?

Using Behavioral Email Workflows

The bread and butter of any company lies in generating repeat sales and staying in front of a client. The easiest way to be present is through email marketing. Most people outside of the industry don't realize how much you can customize email campaigns to engage with your followers and build a strong brand.

The first step is making a name for your email and establishing a brand behind it. Instead of calling it the "(Company) Newsletter" have some fun with it. Find something unique and interesting such as:

- Coffee Business – *The Daily Roast*
- Content Writing Business – *The Next Draft*
- App Review Company – *You Bet Your App*

Having trouble being creative? Below are some alternatives to the word "newsletter" you can use to name your weekly emails:

Bulletin	Chronicle
Publication	Memo
eMagazine	News Page
Journal	Download
Daily	Editorial
Weekly	Snapshot
Monthly	Sentences
Report	Words
Inside Look	Pages

Once you have a name for your email "newsletter," it's important to send out content that your subscribers will find valuable and look forward to receiving. Cram as much value as possible into your email and always provide a link back to your website. Some topic ideas you can use to keep your subscribers from hitting the spam button are:

Before and After: Showing your subscribers simple before and after pics with a quick summary of how the transformation happened is a fool proof way to get your open rate up and to provide proof that your service can do what you claim.

Some examples of Before and After ideas would be:

- Screenshots of sales revenue before and after working with you
- Website Make Over, Before and After
- Credit Score, 64 Point improvement in 48 Hours

Exposing Secrets: Let's be honest; everyone wants a short cut, and if your email offers subscribers a little known secret (regarding their area of interest), they will be more likely to check it out.

- 5 Secrets to Building Massive Email Lists
- The Best Kept Secret in Writing Sales Copy
- The #1 Secret to Becoming Financially Independent

Staying Topical: This technique has been around for a long time. In many marketing circles it's referred to as "News Jacking." News Jacking uses current events to draw attention to your message.

- Our Motor Oil is Thicker Than Kim Kardashian
- How to Impeach Your Competitors Off Google Results
- Why Lil Wayne Refuses to Wear Sandals

Once you have a name and copy, the next step is to sign up for an email service provider so you can customize the way your emails are being sent. This process is called "Setting Up Workflows" and allows you to send different emails to different subscribers depending on the actions they take. For example, if someone opens an email but doesn't click the link to the offer, you want to treat him/her very differently from someone who never opened the email at all.

At the time I am writing this, I like Mailchimp over the more expensive options out there because they have much higher learning curves. Once you feel you have maxed out the capabilities of Mailchimp, move to a full inbound marketing platform like HubSpot.

Hosting Free Webinars & Workshops

Hosting webinars and workshops takes a decent commitment of time to do correctly, but have (by far) the highest upside of any available engagement. Inviting your followers to hear you talk live about something they are interested in is a big draw, and if you dial in your topic and content, you can energize a big percentage of your base. In this section I am going to explain the importance of webinars for your AIS and how you can avoid many of the pitfalls people face when organizing them.

Main Goals of a Webinar

Your webinar should be divided into two sections: educating and selling. Let's assume you are doing a standard, one-hour webinar or workshop. You should devote the first 30 minutes to getting your audience excited and sharing valuable educational information related to the issue your AIS solves. This is your chance to show your audience your tremendous industry knowledge and to convince them you have real solid info to share. By the end of the 30 minutes your audience should be in awe of the value you just gave them and they will want more. At the halfway mark, you switch gears and start showing them how much your AIS could help streamline the entire process.

I know this may sound confusing to everyone who has never hosted a webinar before, so I will break down how I used this process for my LinkedIn Marketing AIS.

I hosted a free webinar on how to generate over 1,000,000 views organically on a LinkedIn post without spending a dime. I went in-depth, showing my audience how I research the content I think will trend, simple tricks I used to bump me up in the algorithm, several free tools I employed to create quick custom content, etc. My viewers were deeply engaged and I could tell by the questions that everyone was really excited to log out of the webinar and test some of the new strategies.

This was when I hit them with the next phase of the webinar: how I could easily generate thousands of new connections and dozens of high-quality warm leads for them each week for less than $5 a day. By the time I went into my pitch, I had already proven my expertise and that I'd been successfully doing this for years. I know the majority of my audience really didn't want more views on their posts; they wanted more leads off LinkedIn. I gave them a perfect solution, one they understood because of the first half of the webinar.

Webinar Tips and Tricks

Be Positive: Half the reason webinars are so effective is because of the attitude and vibe you give off during the presentation. If you aren't excited, your audience will remain flat and unengaged. Always be high energy and speak with passion about your subject.

Focus on Free: Make an interesting title that focuses on what the attendee will be learning in the webinar. This is often referred to as "The Big Promise" and shouldn't be more than a few words. Examples of Big Promise Headlines:

- How to (Do Something) Like a Boss
- 10 Little Known Ways to (Do Something)
- How to Double Your (Something) Without Any Extra Work
- (Topic) 101: Be a Pro at (topic) in 7 Days

Use Trial Closes: Trial closes have been a staple of salesmen for decades – because they work. Think of a trial close as a way of gauging the audience's interest and setting up the sale. If you keep asking questions that get the client to respond positively, you have a much better chance of closing the lead at the end of the webinar. My personal favorite Trial Closes:

- Isn't it cool that (name) made ($xxxx) in just 30 days?
- Can you imagine never worrying about (problem your service is solving)?
- What is your time worth? Should you spend your time on (doing something) when you can pay a few bucks a day never to think about it?

Generating Referrals

If you're doing your job right, your followers will be singing your praises and telling their friends about your AIS. Building a great service and providing real value to your clients will build you organic, word-of-mouth referrals that money literally cannot buy. Those referrals are yours to lose. These come from going above and beyond for your client, providing a good value, being honest, and taking client needs seriously.

The biggest and best referral I ever got was through my school. One of the school leaders knew of my work and referred me to a company that specialized in buying and selling for-profit schools. I was paid to help the school that was for sale get better rankings. The folks in charge also asked me to analyze whether there was enough room in the industry, in the local markets, to complete. The services expanded. They said, "This school does a terrible job at marketing, but there's not much competition. You think, if we buy the school, we can get ten times the social media and online exposure in one year."

"Yes, I can," I said – and I charged accordingly.

That one referral helped me pay back my student debt of $40,000 + ten-fold.

While the random, free, inbound referral is great, I find it's usually a good idea to offer my current clients an incentive to throw some business my way.

Building a Referral Program

If you aren't utilizing technology to generate referrals, you will quickly discover you are wasting a massive amount of time and energy managing relationships and answering questions – for minimal return. To prevent this from happening, build out an affiliate portal and direct all your questions, comments, and concerns back to the platform.

I use an app called "ReferralCandy," which automatically tracks your leads and pays out commissions. The software is $49 a month, but allows me to build the portal using my own branding and tiered referrals. The site is not limited to cash; I can give away coupons or customized gifts as well.

How to Generate Referrals

Affiliate Partners: The quickest and easiest way is to post your AIS in affiliate portals (such as CJ.com that allows digital marketers to sell your product for a percent of the sale).
Ping Your List: Send out emails once a month asking your members if they know of anyone looking for the solution that your AIS offers, and offering them something for every successful close. A good friend of mine, Michael Mogill from Crisp Video Group, has used this model to generate a massive amount of referral business. Of course, he is also giving away Teslas and Ferraris as incentives.

Referral Tips and Tricks

Non-Monetary Rewards: It's a big misconception that you need to give a large percent of the sale to someone for referring you to a friend. Don't forget – most people are just happy to refer someone to you because they were impressed with the service you provided. I find it's better to give someone something with thought and meaning behind it than a lavish gift. When someone makes a referral, I will go to their Facebook page and see what their hobbies are, then send something indicating that I took the time to learn a little about them. I also find that non-monetary rewards can be more valuable to people than a cash prize. It might be something they want, but can't buy, like a vacation.

Game-ify Referrals: This is a great thing to add to a website. Basically, it's a pop-up where if someone enters their email, or the email of a friend, they win a chance at a prize. Let's say, $20, $30 or $50 or Nothing! You can control it, and make sure it always falls on $20, for example – so, that they're not receiving the top prize, but they are getting something for giving you a valid email address of someone who might become a lead or referral.

Promoting Social Media Shares: You can give away virtual tickets or points for shares on Facebook, Instagram, or other social media sites. People who help you can also get tickets or points for legitimate email referrals. You're using your own traffic to go viral. And, it can all be automated via a wide variety of apps and programs. You'd be surprised how often people will share your content, every day, just for the chance of winning 15 tickets/entries!
Note: If you haven't read it I would highly recommend my good friend John Ruhlin's book, *Giftology,* which gives great advice on gifting strategy.

Utilizing Contests & Giveaways

Everyone likes free stuff. Even if there's just a small chance of someone winning something for free, people will take time out of their day to engage. Thanks to social media, your contest can go viral overnight, generating thousands of entries a day.

For example, for one of my recent referral giveaways, I'm giving away a vacation to a beachfront resort (a client) and including a $200 or $300 voucher toward airfare. The client simply has to send someone to me and then pick a resort in the Dominican Republic or Mexico. It's still cost effective for me since I'm working with my partners and I'm sending someone on vacation who will only have to spend a couple hundred bucks out of pocket to enjoy a great vacation.

Reflection

What Before and After's are you most proud of? What are some new ones you could show off?

_____
_____
_____
_____

What can you make a webinar about, and how can you best market it to your audience?

_____
_____
_____
_____

What are you currently doing to generate referrals? What should you do more?

_____
_____
_____
_____

"Content Marketing is no longer a numbers game. It's a game of relevance."

Jason Miller

Chapter 7

Increasing Life-Time Value (LTV)

No matter what service or product you sell, you need an upsell to maximize the profitability of the business. It's much easier to sell something else once the customer has just completed a purchase. Many people would be shocked to learn that many businesses rely solely on the upselling to generate profit on a sale. Here are some great examples of how I have used upsells in my various AIS projects:

eCom AIS

Breathalyzer Keychains: This was my first real AIS business, and one we talked about earlier in this book. To be honest, I made a lot of mistakes – but I also learned a lot of core lessons I would use for the next 15 years. My upsell was simple: if you bought a breathalyzer keychain, I would give the option to buy three refills for 50% off. Because these were single-use breathalyzers, people buying the refills were around 40%. What would I have done differently? Looking back, I should have found another higher margin product to sell after the breathalyzers were purchased.

Neon Signs: Eye flow neon signs was my second eCom venture. I found a guy on eBay who was making solar powered neon yard signs for realtors and knew I could sell a boatload of them. We worked out a paper napkin partnership agreement and I went to work building sites. The sales started rolling in. My margins were slim, and the production was limited as it was just two guys making these signs by hand. So, I quickly realized I needed to add an upsell or move on to the next venture.

My first upsell was a lifetime warranty. I knew the products were well made and would last a long time unless there was physical damage. I sold the signs for $99 and had an optional lifetime warranty for $49. The best part was that I got my partner to agree to a lifetime warranty, so there was no extra cost on my end. I just added $49 to my bottom line.

The next upsell was submitting the customers to 100+ national real estate directories. You might laugh now, but back in the early 2000's, directories were huge and everyone wanted to be in as many as they could. I had a small digital marketing company with some partners in India, so it was easy to offer a low-cost (yet high perceived value) service. Instead of asking for another big payment upfront, I offered 50+ directory submissions for $9.99 a month – no contract, no commitment, and they could quit anytime. This was a gold mine as the process was 100% automated by submission software, and I was paying around $1 a month. In fact, the concept was so profitable I started lowering the price of the signs just to get more submission business, which I would then upsell into my digital marketing agency.

WUDN: By the time I launched WUDN I had managed tens of millions in digital ad spend. Software also caught up. Instead of having to spend thousands on custom created software solutions, you could buy something off the shelf for $10 that was 100x more effective.

The first real hit I had with WUDN was for the wooden iPhone battery case I wrote about earlier. Up to that point, the only battery cases you could get for your phone were cheap looking, black plastic bricks. We slapped some wood veneer on the outside, put up some ads, and started getting tens of thousands of views a day. It was something to see. We were paying a few dollars for a case and selling them for $50+ just by adding what was essentially a wood sticker to an existing product. We would not keep up and had to quadruple our machinery in a month to keep our heads above water on orders. As we grew, competitors started making similar products and we had to cut costs to compete, we started taking our upsells more seriously.

The first upsell product was a self-adhesive glass cover that looked amazing when it was applied. It almost looked like something from the future, the way the glass just sucked onto the phone. We priced it at $39.99 on the site, but if you bought it within 15 minutes of buying your case, you could get it for $14.99. Our cost was around 75 cents.

Whether or not you bought the glass upsell, you were also prompted to purchase our Bluetooth headphones. Normally they sold at $59.99, but if you bought within 15 minutes of getting the phone case, you could get them for $19.99. Our cost was $3.

Reflection

What are some ideas you have for an upsell?

_____
_____
_____
_____

What are the pros and cons of each idea?

_____
_____
_____
_____

How can you use upsells to maximize the profitability of your business?

_____
_____
_____
_____

"We need to stop interrupting what people are interested in and be what people are interested in."

David Beebe

Bonus Chapter

Miscellaneous Thoughts on Digital Platforms

At the end of the day, marketing is what makes the world spin and a successful entrepreneur knows that the right marketing campaign can sell even the most useless product or service.

Let's take a look at how to use various digital platforms to market *any* product or service to your audience in a way designed to make them not just customers but also loyal brand advocates.

Setting Up Bots

The one thing I hope you have learned at this point is that automation is one of the most important aspects of making passive income. In this section I am going to show you some automated bots you can set up to prospect for new business daily passively. Because, let's face it, in today's world, technology can completely transform a business.

Working with an automated script, bots can take a massive amount of time off your hands. We use bots for our marketing. We send customized messages to people who follow or like our Instagram account – we've used them through LinkedIn as well.

Maybe the bot offers something for free or asks a question. Maybe the bot is trained to begin a conversation. Once the target engages, and before he realizes he's talking to a machine, you jump in and take over. You can transform a "cool," relatively generic interchange into a "warm," engaging conversation.

There are also email bots that can send out specific, customized emails based on plugged-in information. When someone responds, the bot "cuts out" and you step in. If someone "likes" a photo on your Instagram site, a chat bot will send them a quick note – maybe thanking them for the like and asking if they want more information

Some of these bots can be fully automated or you can keep their interaction simply – more of a "yes/no" situation. As your profile grows, you won't have time to respond to every like or comment, but your bot can. It's a tough balance, though. You want to be authentic and if people sniff a bot, they'll run a mile a minute away from you and what you offer. So, I suggest using bots to gather tiny bits of information to establish a bigger picture of you – to build a wider presence. Handle all the conversations yourself.

LinkedIn: Dux Soup

I've used LinkedIn to prospect (passively) up to 500 targeted people daily. This costs around $50 a month but is well worth the investment. What's great about the strategy is you will passively get your message in front of key decision makers and – here's the great part – they contact you.

Step #1: Buy and install Dux Soup in your browser

Step #2: Change your LinkedIn job title to a description of your service i.e. "I Can Streamline your Accounting for $250 a month," "I help Companies Generate Thousands of *Real* Followers for $199 a month," "Giving Away Free Customized H.R. Handbooks – DM me"

Step #3: Change your header image to something with a clear call to action and ensure it predominantly displays your contact info.

Step #4: Choose your target market and hit "start." The software will automatically visit hundreds of profiles a day and since LinkedIn displays your job title in the "Who Viewed Your Profile," your CTA will be showing up in tens of thousands of potential clients each month.

Final Thoughts

I love the book, *The Four-Hour Workweek*, by Tim Ferris. That's exactly what we're talking about here with AIS. Reading that book changed my life and made me see that I didn't *have* to work 40 or more hours a week to make a good living. I could work 10, 8, 6, and 4 hours a week, as I refined my processes and became an AIS believer.

Tim talks about outsourcing and automating. I hadn't thought about doing that type of business before. I was all hands-on – do everything myself or don't do it. Outsourcing and automating meant giving up control.

Yes. And no.

Sure, you might give up managing the day-to-day, hour-by-hour stuff, but you are actually gaining control. You're managing the direction and focus of your business. You're directing the scope and scale of your business. You're deciding the different ways you can outsource and automate according to the ideas and tips I've included in this book. In many ways, you're taking control of your business and control of your life.

I know I'm no Tim Ferris, but I hope this book changes your life in a very real way. I want you to recognize that you can create an incredible future for yourself using AIS strategies. There's no reason you can't be part of the two percent of people who hears about these types of business models, jumps on them, and sticks with them.

This is not some magic money printing machine. You will have to work. In the beginning, you'll have to work much more than forty hours a week. But, once you get your systems up and running, you can take control of your work week and your life, and build a six or seven-figure business – all from your computer. You can work out of your home with no employee hassles and very few regulations. Better still – you will even earn money while you sleep.

This book is part of a larger program that I'm building. I want to add e-course, worksheets and tools, and much more. Thanks for being a part of our AIS community. I look forward to watching you and your success as you navigate this new and exciting opportunity.

What Do I Do Now?

So, you've gone through the book. Hopefully, you are fired up and ready to get cranking on setting up your first AIS. Let's review the steps.

Research Quality Services

The first step: Go on sites and find a service you feel is underpriced but provides a lot of value to the client. I prefer sites where you can see user reviews of the person/company to verify they have decent experience and customer service. Below are the sites where I have had the most luck finding AIS services:

a. Fiverr.com
b. Upwork.com
c. Freelancer.com

Another way to find a good AIS service is to research cutting edge technology offerings. I have seen folks charge hundreds of dollars for reports they created for free using a new software that isn't widely known yet. Below are some of the sites I use to stay up with new technology:

a. Google Chrome Store: There are amazing Chrome Plugins that can do unlimited actions for a small monthly membership fee.

b. Amazon.com: The biggest advantage of Amazon is the reviews. You can determine the quality of a piece of software very quickly.

c. CodeCanyon.net: There are thousands of cheap, customizable scripts you can rebrand to a niche industry and resell for a massive ROI. I once sold used video game scripts (cost: $30) to sell tens of customizable games to companies to feature their social media/websites.

Pro Tip:

* Stick to industries you know. For example: if you are an artist, stick with graphic/visual services and steer away from financial modeling or analytical jobs.

- **Vet The Service Provider**

  Since you are outsourcing all of the work it's *very* important for you to vet a supplier thoroughly and to verify they will provide exceptional quality and customer support.

  Step 1: Order their service and keep track of everything. *How soon did they start the work? Was it completed on time? How was their communication? Was the service over-promised and under-delivered?*

Step 2: Throw some curveballs at them. When you start offering the service to clients, they will ask for things outside the normal service. You must know how the service provider will respond. If it takes them days to reply to emails or messages, you will smash headfirst into a massive problem at scale.

Pro Tip: Don't get too far outside your wheelhouse where the service is no longer streamlined. Don't be afraid to tell a difficult client you are not going to change your offering just for them. I never tell a client, "I can't do that," but I will offer them a custom quote with the warning that it might cost them substantially more. 99.9% of the time, they won't take the option. If they do, at least you get paid for your time!

- **Build a Minimal Viable Product**

Now that you have a solid service and provider, it's time to test everything. In the industry, we typically ask, Again – "Will the dogs eat the dog food?" You want to build a quick brand and offer promotional materials to present to potential clients. Here are the minimal things you should prepare before approaching anyone.

a. *Build a Brand.* This sounds hard, but since you are just building an MVP, you can just download a brand template and edit it as needed. I like to use Graphic River and search for keywords related to my AIS's industry. You can download an entire professional-looking quickly brand for under $20.

b. *Build a one page website.* You can use a simple site creator or landing page software to get something up in an hour. Take a look at some of these.

Content Management Platforms:
Some Technical Know How:
Shopify
WordPress

No Technical Know How:
Squarespace
Wix

Landing Page Software:
Instapage
Lead Pages
Unbounce

Pro Tip: If you don't feel comfortable building your own site, you can get someone cheap on Fiverr to throw up a quick, templated website.

- **Start Marketing Your Product**

    This is typically the hardest part for new entrepreneurs, so I will try to cram in as much advice and strategy as I can. What makes this difficult is every AIS will be different and every entrepreneur has his/her own strengths and weaknesses. Following, you will find some cheap and easy ways to generate your first leads without approaching friends and family.

    a. Engage In Industry Specific Groups & Forums: One of the quickest ways to get warm inbound leads is to be active in places your potential clients go. Think about what Facebook, LinkedIn, and Google groups your clientele are on and establish yourself as an industry leader. Don't just spam the group looking for sales. Work to be helpful and provide value.

    Pro Tip: Validate what you say by highlighting your accomplishments. Show screen shots of results and describe (in detail) how you solve issues your potential clients will face.

    b. **Targeted Emails:** I never condone mass spamming emails but there are tons of great software to help you send small numbers emails a day to targeted prospects.

The goal lies in offering value to move the recipients to respond. You might try some of the following.

Template Ideas:
- Hey (Name), I've heard your name around (AIS industry) circles and I would love to connect and see if you would be interested in some free consulting on how I can (Make a big promise).

- Hey (Name), I apologize if you're the wrong contact but I was trying to reach out to someone at (company name) to see if anyone would be interested in learning about a new system I developed for local (industry) businesses. It's enjoying a lot of success right now.

Cold Email software:
QuickMail
Mailshake
Reply.io

- **Optimize, Automate, and Monetize**

    After a week or two, you should know if your AIS will sink or swim. If people seem receptive, it's time to scale.

AUTOMATE YOUR INCOME

Automate:

The most alluring thing about an AIS is how much money it can generate without taking hours on a daily basis. It's very important to automate the process and put most of the work on the service provider without revealing your model. I typically ask my service provider to handle customer support via chat with a client on my website. I used to use email but you will have providers go behind your back and cut you out.

Another huge time saver is to make an extensive FAQ or Wiki for clients. This way, one person can answer 90% of questions with a simple copy and paste. Every time you get a new question, add it to the FAQ or the Wiki!

Monetize:

Think of what services you can upsell/cross sell to increase a client's LTV (Long Term Value). I will use a logo design service as an example.

Core Service:

Logo Design

Upsells:

Upsells are designed to encourage someone to pull the trigger on another purchase at the point of sale. It is always easier to convince someone to buy something "at check out" than to "sell" them again in the future. Pick a low-cost buy/high-margin service. In the logo design field, you can use: 3D Mock Up, different file formats & resolutions, letterhead & stationery design, more design variations, email signatures, etc.

Cross Sells:

Cross sells are typically more expensive. They complement your core offering. If you were selling a logo design service, it's safe to assume you are working with a startup company. You might cross sell web design, content writing, SEO, paid advertising, social media management, etc.

- **Plan Your next AIS!**
  You will learn and grow with every AIS you build. Don't get disappointed when the first one or two aren't profitable. Learn from your mistakes - and do better on the next one.

  Well everyone, I think that's about as much advice as I can give to get you started. If you want more tips and tricks, you can follow me on your favorite social media channel or visit PhilLaboon.com to see what I'm up to.

Remember, If you hit a snag, reach out! I live and breathe this stuff - I never get tired of talking about it, so don't be afraid to holler

P.S. - I shut down and recover over the weekends - the advantage of passive income!

Testimonials

"I've worked with Phil for years and have been involved in several of his automated businesses streams and all I can say is, 'Wow!' Phil's brain doesn't work like the average entrepreneur's and he has a unique uncanny ability to identify and implement quickly."

Chad Keller
Co-Founder
MarketerHire.com

"Phil is the real deal! I've partnered with him on creating an automated income stream that pulls in over $70,000 a year with only a few hours of maintenance a week. I've learned more in a few months working with Phil than I did in four years at college and I'm already working on developing several of my own streams for 2020!"

Mike Moore
CEO
LinkedStacker.com

"I originally met Phil when I approached him to do marketing for my start-up concept. In only one meeting he was able to reconstruct and simplify my entire monetization model. Within one year of launching the model, my business began to generate a seven-figure profit with no employees and no office."

Bryan Liposky
Co-Founder
USADiscounts.com

www.ingramcontent.com/pod-product-compliance
Lightning Source LLC
Chambersburg PA
CBHW071413210526
45465CB00001B/363